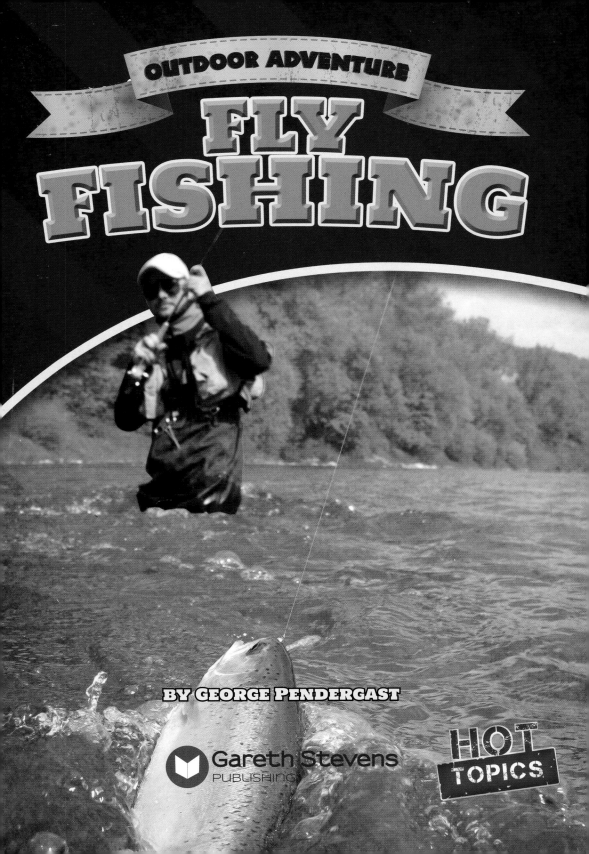

OUTDOOR ADVENTURE

FLY FISHING

BY GEORGE PENDERGAST

Gareth Stevens
PUBLISHING

HOT TOPICS

Please visit our website, www.garethstevens.com. For a free color catalog of all our high-quality books, call toll free 1-800-542-2595 or fax 1-877-542-2596.

Pendergast, George.
Fly fishing / by George Pendergast.
p. cm. — (Outdoor adventure)
Includes index.
ISBN 978-1-4824-1229-1 (pbk.)
ISBN 978-1-4824-1236-9 (6-pack)
ISBN 978-1-4824-1492-9 (library binding)
1. Fly fishing — Juvenile literature. I. Title.
SH456.P46 2015
799.12—d23

First Edition

Published in 2015 by
Gareth Stevens Publishing
111 East 14th Street, Suite 349
New York, NY 10003

Designer: Nick Domiano
Editor: Ryan Nagelhout

Photo credits: Cover, p. 1 Peter Zachar/Shutterstock.com; cover texture Yuriy Boyko/ Shutterstock.com; cover ribbon blinkblink/Shutterstock.com; pp. 4-5 Corey Hochachka/ Design Pics/Getty Images; pp. 6-7 Matt Jeppson/Shutterstock.com; pp. 8-9, 24-25 Sean Boggs/E+/Getty Images; p. 11 John Burke/Photolibrary/Getty Images; pp. 12-13 Sandra Cunningham/Shutterstock.com; pp. 14-15 Bplanet/Shutterstock.com; pp. 16-17 David Epperson/Photodisc/Getty Images; pp. 18-19 Areipa.it/Shutterstock.com; pp. 20-21 Jacom Stephens/Vetta/Getty Images; p. 23 © iStockPhoto.com/joshuaraineyphotography; pp. 26-27 Peter Zachar/Shutterstock.com; p. 29 Alistair Berg/Digital Vision/Getty Images; p. 30 (fly lure) kzww/Shutterstock.com; p. 30 (life jacket) objectsforall/Shutterstock.com.

Printed in the United States of America

CPSIA compliance information: Batch #CS15GS: For further information contact Gareth Stevens, New York, New York at 1-800-542-2595.

CONTENTS

ON THE FLY

Many people love to fish. One great way to catch some fish is to go fly fishing. Fly fishing is easy to learn and lots of fun!

People go fly fishing all over the world. They fish in freshwater streams and lakes. You can even fly fish in salt water. People like to catch lots of different fish.

LEARN TO FISH

People usually learn to fish with live **bait**. They use a fishing pole and bait along with a weight called a bobber. The bobber is used to throw the line far. The bobber also lets a fisherman see how far the line was thrown.

Fly fishing is a bit different from fishing with a bobber. You need special gear to fly fish. Fly fishermen use special fishing rods called fly rods. They're usually made of strong things like **metal** or **bamboo**.

ON THE LINE

Fly rods use something called a fly line instead of a bobber. The fly line is a strong string that is tied around a **reel** at the base of the pole. The reel keeps the fly line from getting tangled.

13

SKINNY WEIGHT

The fly line acts like a long, skinny weight. Fly fisherman pull the line from the reel. Next, the rod is pulled back and thrown forward. The more fly line you pull out, the farther the bait will go.

Any fish that eats bugs can be caught using a fly rod. A fly fisherman tries to make the bait look like a bug on top of the water. Most fishermen make the bait jump back and forth, just like a fly!

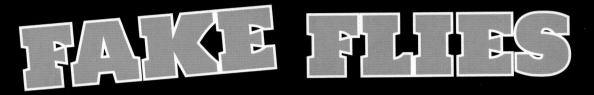

FAKE FLIES

There are many different ways to bait a fish. Most people don't use live bugs. Fly fishermen like to use fake flies! Flies come in many different sizes, colors, and shapes.

To pick out the right fly, you need to know what different fish eat. Many people go fly fishing with guides to help them use the right bait. Guides also help them find places where lots of fish swim!

RIGGING IT RIGHT

The types of bait and fly line a fisherman uses are called a rig. Fly fishermen make their rigs in different ways. Some tie their line in special shapes to make round **loops**. Others tie **knots** in their line to keep their hooks and bait in place.

When a fish takes the bait, fly fishermen reel them in! Some people like to keep the fish they catch. Some fishermen even eat them. Many fly fishermen like to catch fish and throw them back in the water. This is called catch-and-release fishing.

WADING IN

Many people like to stand in water when they fly fish. This is called **wading**. Fly fishermen wear big boots to stay dry. They have to be very careful when they wade in water. You don't want to get stuck in the water!

PRACTICE MAKES PERFECT

Fly fishing is a great way to relax and catch some fish. All you need are a few trips out on the water, and you'll be catching fish in no time. Just make sure you stay safe!

FLY FISHING SAFETY

- Always use a wading staff in the water.
- Wear a life jacket when on a boat.
- Wear proper gear like wading boots in water.
- Don't leave equipment on the ground.
- Be careful with hooks.
- Cast pole away from others.
- Don't cast toward other objects.

FOR MORE INFORMATION

Books

Crockett, Sally. *Fly Fishing*. New York, NY: Rosen Central, 2012.

Jenson-Elliott, Cynthia L. *Fly Fishing*. Mankato, MN: Capstone Press, 2012.

Pound, Blake. *Fly Fishing*. Minneapolis, MN: Bellwether Media, 2013.

Websites

Fly Fishing Guides

takekidsflyfishing.com/2011/04/kid-friendly-fly-fishing-guides
Find kid-friendly guides who will take you fly fishing today!

Fly Fishing Video Lessons

howtoflyfish.orvis.com/video-lessons
Watch videos and learn how to fly fish with these step-by-step guides.

Take Kids Fly Fishing

takekidsflyfishing.com
Learn more about fly-fishing gear and ways to catch fish on this great site.

GLOSSARY

bait: something used to attract another animal

bamboo: a very strong woody grass

knot: a tie of line or string that creates a lump

loop: a fold of a line or string that makes a space for something to pass through

metal: a hard, shiny matter found in the ground

reel: a tool that is turned to gather fishing line, or to collect a fishing line

wade: to step in or through water or mud

INDEX